SUM

by Susan Gray

Published by Playdead Press 2014

© Susan Gray

Susan Gray has asserted her rights under the Copyright, Design and Patents Act, 1988, to be identified as the author of this work.

A CIP catalogue record for this book is available from the British Library.

ISBN 978-1-910067-27-7

Caution
All rights whatsoever in this play are strictly reserved and application for performance should be sought through the author before rehearsals begin. No performance may be given unless a license has been obtained.

This book is sold subject to the condition that it shall not by way of trade or otherwise, be lent, resold, hired out, or otherwise circulated without the publisher's prior consent in any form of binding or cover other than that in which it is published and without a similar condition including this condition being imposed on the subsequent purchaser.

Playdead Press
www.playdeadpress.com

Sum was first performed at Bread and Roses Theatre, London on 27th November 2014 with the following cast:

Cast:

Briony Wyatt
Eleanor Russo
Lydia Kay
Melanie Crossey
Susan Gray

Creative and Production Team:

Susan Gray	Writer/Producer
Chris Callow Jr.	Director
Lucy Ann Harrison	Sound designer

Cast Biographies

Briony Wyatt

Briony trained at Drama Studio London. Her recent credits include *Terra Firma by Susan Gray* (Camden Fringe), *An Evening of the Absurd: Are We All Still Waiting For Godot?* a devised piece (Camden Fringe Festival) and *Unpicking the Seams of Reality*, an immersive dinner theatre show. She is also a voice over artist specialising in corporate voice work.

Eleanor Russo

Eleanor trained at Drama Studio London. Credits include: "Ophelia" in *Hamlet* (Network Theatre and International Tour), "Journalist" in *Bugsy Malone* (Future Cinema), "Lily" in *Postscript* (Theatre 503), "Dol Common" in *The Alchemist* (Rose Theatre, Bankside), "Margaret" in *Muscovado* (Clapham Omnibus), "Rachel" in *Terra Firma* (Etcetera Theatre). Eleanor is a bilingual English/Italian actress.

Lydia Kay

British actress born in Leighton Buzzard, Bedfordshire. Lydia started performing at the age of six with local dramatics group Leighton Buzzard Children's Theatre, and later graduated from East 15 Acting School. Since then Lydia has been in numerous independent films including *Survivors*, *Christmas Slay* and *Invasion of the Not Quite Dead*. She performed throughout the London 2012 Olympic and Paralympic Games, has taken to the stage for both touring pantomime and interactive theatre, and become a professional scare actor working in numerous mazes at both Thorpe Park and Madame Tussaud's London. She is also the founder of #ActingHour on Twitter, which is a way for those involved in all aspects of the industry to get their work seen by more people and to create networking and work opportunities.

Melanie Crossey
With beginnings as a young girl primarily as a dancer and musician, Melanie soon moved into acting. After graduating with a degree in Performing Arts from Bath Spa University, she toured Italy for 8 months in various productions for Lingue Senza Frontiere. Having discovered a major passion for film, this has been her main focus for the past few years. Recent credits include: *Holland Park* (Dir. Kenan Akbulut), *Rite of Passage* (Dir. Sacha Allari), *PIOUS* (Dir. Joseph Buchanan), *One Flew Over The Hornet's Nest* (Dir. Natasha Cosila Luchmun) and the recently released Sci Fi short *SYNC* (Dir. Hasraf Dulull)

Susan Gray
Susan Gray is a writer, performer and 3rd year PhD student of Creative Writing. She has performed spoken word at the Roundhouse, Camden, the Free Word Centre in Farringdon and the Poetry Cafe in Covent Garden. Acting credits include: *The Norman Conquests* (Brunel University), *Off With Her Head!* (Brockwell Park), *The Greatest Poet who Ever Lived* (Roundhouse Poetry Collective, Edinburgh Festival) and *The Happiest Time of the Year* (Writers Bloc, The Old Red Lion Theatre). She has also performed and read her

monologues from her recently published book *Notes from Other Worlds* (2014) at the Centre for Creative Collaboration in Kings Cross.

Creative Biographies

Chris Callow Jr. | Director

Chris Callow Jr studied acting at the Drama School "Athenian Stage" in Greece, followed by an MA in Playwriting at UCLAN, and he has recently completed a PhD in Creative Writing at Birkbeck, University of London. This is the 2nd play he directs.

Lucy Ann Harrison | Sound Designer

Lucy creates interactive sound installations and sound design for theatre. She studied music and composition at Durham University before moving to pursue a PhD in composition, studying with Brian Lock at Royal Holloway.

Previous theatre work has included *The Mariam Project* (Burford Festival 2013), *The Carey Cycles* at The "Gretchen Day" (Gallery Peckham 2013) and *The Massacre* (Dilston Grove 2014).

Large scale installations include 'The Wind Singer' based on the book by William Nicholson and 'That I Will Do My Best...' for Girl Guiding's World Thinking Day 2014.

Lucy is a member of *Written and Composed* where she collaborates with Susan Gray.

Examples of Lucy's work can be found at laharrisonmusic.co.uk

Susan Gray | Writer

Susan Gray is a writer/performer based in Harrow, North London. She is currently researching Science Fiction Theatre as part of her PhD in Creative Writing and Practice Based in Royal Holloway, University of London. Previous Writing Credits include: *A Christmas Gift* (Old Red Lion Theatre), *Newshound* (Brockley Jack Theatre) *Cuckoos and Chrysalides* (Old Red Lion Theatre), *The Reality Test* (Old Red Lion Theatre), *Terra Firma* (Etcetera Theatre) and Lock Up your Skeletons (KDC Theatre at The Hoop and Grapes). Her SF monologues collection, Notes from Other Worlds, was published by Playdead Press.

Stars or Mars Theatre
www.starsormarstheatre.co.uk

Stars or Mars is a theatre company based in London, which is dedicated to new writing in the Science Fiction genre.

Whilst Science Fiction has always been included in Theatre, it is an arguably marginalised art - to the point where people can be hard pressed to name a Science Fiction play. It is usually either listed under a comedy or parody - lacking the visual detail of the more popular Science Fiction Film and Television media.

Stars or Mars believes that Science Fiction can be staged first and foremost through the human - with no reason for special effects. The use of language and physicality can portray these alternate worlds, especially where our reality is becoming increasingly compromised by technologies.

Previous work includes: *Newshound* (Brockley Jack Theatre), *Terra Firma* (Etcetera Theatre) and *Notes from Other Worlds* (Centre for Creative Collaboration).

Our company is writer-led: telling stories far from home, but close to the bone.

Artistic Director: Susan Gray

The Bread & Roses Theatre
www.BreadandRosesTheatre.co.uk

The Bread & Roses Theatre is a pub theatre in Clapham, South London, located above the Bread & Roses pub.

The venue programs a wide-spread variety of productions and aims to provide theatre-makers with a space to develop and present their work.

Located in Clapham, within walking distance of several tube and overground stations in Zone 2 (Clapham North, Clapham Common, Clapham High Street and Wandsworth Road), the theatre sits in a brilliant location.

It is also home of the in-house Bread & Roses Theatre Company, which focuses on supporting new and contemporary writing. The venue is run by fellow theatre-makers on a voluntary basis; it is managed by Tessa Hart and Rebecca Pryle.

Staff:
Tessa Hart - Venue Co-Manager/ Web Designer/ Box Office
Rebecca Pryle - Venue Co-Manager/Company Manager
Grace Dunne - Company Member
Hannah Duffy - Company Member

Characters:

SAM
PI
CARRIE (LAN)
SYNE
LAW

ACT I

Scene 1

PI and SAM are sitting, facing the audience.

PI	Have faith in the pilot, right?
SAM	That's all you can do.
[beat]	
	They seemed alright, didn't they?
PI	If you call lying still under plastic sheeting "alright"/
SAM	/they were breathing perfectly well!
PI	And you were present at the scene with a stethoscope?
SAM	I was there. You can see breathing.
PI	Fine.
SAM	We're not the first. They know what to do now. When it comes to us, it won't look as sinister.
PI	I damn hope so!
[beat]	
	You're remarkably calm.
SAM	Problem?

PI	There's such a thing as being too calm.
SAM	Nah, not in this situation. If you know what's going to happen, then what's the problem?
PI	But you chose this.
SAM	So did you.

[beat]

> This is a voluntary program. No matter what our positions going into it. It doesn't matter. That's the point - we're the same going in, going out.

[beat]

PI	We're not going to be the same going out though, that's the point!
SAM	I'd rather take the chance in here than an inevitable death out there, in that war zone. Hell, I'd prefer the plastic sheeting.
PI	I know, I know. It's just... the mystery of it. Who's going to connect you, what to expect and/
SAM	/You didn't check your list?

[beat]

PI	What, and you did?

SAM What did you expect?

[beat]

PI It's a plan, Sam - a romantic damn notion. But for us, it's everything. A chance for us to survive, to be safe from all the crap outside. For them it's just some pawns from the system. I have nothing but... ideas. Alternatives. It doesn't seem so real when it's in your head... but on a screen/

SAM /You mean the device of choice for the wiring?

PI You know, I wanted something to be quick.

SAM Just be glad that we have the choice for the tool.

PI But that's the thing! A tool. The method is so... invasive. This is why I'm so scared. I'm scared but excited, of course. When I hid under that shelter, hearing those explosions, I knew I was brought into this world alone, I made others leave it and I'd leave it, alone. All for nothing. Not understanding why people would... why people could... it doesn't make sense. If I could just have reasoned with them - directly...

SAM You don't know how many times I've thought that as well. And that's why we're here - we're holding on, yes, but we could start something amazing.

[beat]

I'm doing this with you. That's for sure.

PI But knowing who's going to connect you - won't that make it worse?

SAM Depends, really, doesn't it? How you react to... surprises.

[beat]

PI I can react well to most surprises. But to know I'm running into enemy fire and know it's homing in for me... fine, not that dramatic.

[beat]

Look. I read up on this stuff, sure - to the point where I was bloated on it. It wasn't enough.

[beat]

Trusting. That's the thing.

SAM Being connected, yes. It's a damn big thing. We can get through it.

PI I know I'm petrified. I know. But this could be a way of... trusting people again. Just speaking to you helps. Knowing someone

	could be here and know they wouldn't kill me. Being on the same wavelength – I would do anything. Anything.
SAM	Can you imagine? You'd probably make me laugh on cue like a puppet! I'd be able to make you quiet by just thinking. How amazing would that be?
PI	Sam, I'm serious. I'm just scared about that leap. What if we don't even recognise each other after it all?
[beat]	
SAM	Right. I'm going to do an exercise with you. Just start, start with one.
PI	Exercise?
SAM	Probably not in the way you're thinking! Bloody hell.
PI	Just tell me.
SAM	Needy, aren't you?
[beat]	
	It's for team-building.
PI	Which one? There are a lot out there.
[beat]	
SAM	Get up and walk over here.

PI　　　　　　　Why?

SAM　　　　　　You're questioning, Pi! Typical, huh? All these thoughts, yet we're not moving forwards.

PI　　　　　　　I know the old social media never asked/

SAM　　　　　　/the whole point of trust is not asking these questions. You should know the logistics.

PI　　　　　　　Well, I guess that makes sense, doesn't/

SAM　　　　　　*(amused)* /you're going to make that a question, weren't you? Typical.

PI　　　　　　　Speak for yourself.

[beat]

PI sighs, walks over to the far corner.

PI　　　　　　　Do you like this place?

SAM　　　　　　Question!

PI　　　　　　　I think this is a hospitable environment. As much as a shelter can be. This room is always nicer, isn't it? Much more serene than our quarters, that's for sure. Probably to calm us down before this all happens.

[beat]

SAM	That's a good opinion to have about all of this. Since it's the thing that's keeping us in here. Keeping us afloat.
PI	Argh! Why do you need to bring that up!?
SAM	What?
PI	Question! Haha!

[beat]

	OK, I'll keep it down in here.
SAM	It won't matter soon. Now look, here, stand in front of me, and fall back. I'll catch you.
PI	Oh! That bloody thing!
SAM	It's the only one I know.
PI	Hah! This'll be a cinch!
SAM	Good to know.

[beat]

PI stands behind SAM, who waits for PI to fall. PI does so successfully.

SAM	Look at that! Plain sailing.
PI	I wonder if anyone else has had to... you know/

SAM stabs PI with a syringe.

BLACKOUT.

SAM Everyone's doing it. That's what they'll say when they'll try to lure you in. Actually, no. They won't say it, you'll just know. Their eyes will glaze over when you say you're singular. You'll know what they're thinking. Like, their face is struggling, just like when you're trying to hold in your distaste. But for me it feels like a reverse snobbery, that kind of thing. You know, that you feel that you're so superior for not wanting to belong to one arc, like/

PI/SAM /one of me is worth ten of you/

SAM /and I'm a futurist. I know this will happen. I imagine those in the past would be shocked that people shared everything in such a precarious object as a cloud. No motifs, no symbols - just that. The information. If we all laid down our cards, properly, then there is a perfect game. There will be no game. That's what our lives will be.

ACT 1

Scene 2

PI and SAM are standing in the corners of the stage. CARRIE is sitting on a chair, facing us, the audience.

PI	Not the best place for it.
SAM	For us, you mean?
PI	Does it feel that our biases are levelling out? I have a bad feeling about this.
SAM	Be glad we're not stuck forever in here, because that would be hell. For sure.
[beat]	
	Also, *you* have a bad feeling about this?
PI	Don't be pedantic.
SAM	Just saying.
PI	My time wasn't easy!
SAM	We know that. Believe us!
PI	Well, it's not knowing how it's going to be. There isn't a manual on it. I'm... still not used to it.
SAM	Give that time.
PI	Humans are like that. Irrational. It's hard for them to adapt.

SAM	Excuses.
PI	Those too.
[beat]	
	They're not going down without a fight. Their expectations are different from ours.
SAM	Their expectations?
PI	Singulars. In this case, singular criminals.
SAM	Crime is an exercise of context. Same with singulars. Everyone expects death. No matter what.
PI	So blunt, aren't you? It's not death, though, is it? You still think and move. It's just the way you see yourself is gone. A social death.
SAM	It's the closest thing to it. Oh, and by the way, that bluntness is part of you.
PI	Of us, you mean. Hah!
SAM	We're all bound to slip now and again.
PI	Thinking of new pronouns, new words - it's exciting. It's also good to split up and wander like that.
SAM	But do you know if you're wandering?
PI	Not all who wander/
SAM	/are lost.

PI　　　　　　　You know I wanted to say it at the right time!

[beat]

PI/SAM　　　　You can if you want.

[beat]

PI　　　　　　　It's this speaking our thoughts aloud - it's all so new to me.

SAM　　　　　　It's for Carrie's/

PI　　　　　　　/Not out loud! Sheesh! Like Carrie hasn't realised that herself.

SAM　　　　　　We have to show her that she can still talk. It's an extension of talking to yourself. You know. What those kids used to do on social mediums.

PI　　　　　　　Social media.

SAM　　　　　　I was going to self-correct and/

PI　　　　　　　/It's good to show her we can make mistakes. Still.

SAM　　　　　　That's just the tip of the iceberg.

PI/SAM　　　　It's interesting. To see what pops into your head. Something's good. Something's bad. Wondering where it originated from.

SAM   I remember doing that when I was singular. Was! See!

PI   We were all born singular.

SAM   Will you stop poaching my lines?

PI and SAM walk up to CARRIE and stand next to her, side by side.

PI/SAM   Carrie. Carrie.

CARRIE   I'm not looking.

PI/SAM   There's worse things to be worried about.

[beat]

CARRIE   I don't know. The permanence of it. This is a change I might have to bloody well deal with for the rest of my life. If it damn works.

PI and SAM circle CARRIE.

PI/SAM   The mind often changes. But it's better that than not having one at all.

CARRIE   That's just the way I'm wired.

SAM   How retro is that!

PI   Easy of us to say, huh?

[beat]

	We're not going to kill you. If you go down this route, that is. You won't have to rot away in this cell, will you?
SAM	That wasn't the thing to say. Gosh!
PI	We have to appeal to them with bluntness. Oh, ok then. With truth.
SAM	None of us is dead.

[beat]

CARRIE	It's death in a different sense.
SAM	So that's what change is?
CARRIE	It's a death of something.

[beat]

PI	But you can live on - past the flesh, past that. Knowing that your mind will be connected. Wouldn't you prefer that?
CARRIE	Maybe that was your reason. How do you even know you're the same anymore?
PI	I'm not the same. We're not day to day. But we're on the cusp of something much much bigger than cell regeneration. Believe me.
CARRIE	It's what everyone's wanted, right? Why social media worked. Why this is working. You just need someone to ask the question and one to answer.

SAM　　　　See, you have an inquiring mind! One we'd like to plug into our system.

CARRIE　　But what happens when someone isn't asking the question anymore?

[beat]

PI　　　　And you'd have to tell us. We wouldn't understand exactly what you're trying to say. Can you imagine the time you'd save? The energy, the thinking power?

SAM　　　　Your singular person used to work in marketing, right? No bloody surprise.

[beat]

SAM/PI　　So... we can always come back if you want more time. Or you know, this could be the last/

CARRIE　　/No! I'm in. I've done enough pacing here, for something at sometime someone has deemed as wrong. Bloody bastards.

SAM/PI　　Good answer.

SAM and PI stop and come closer to CARRIE.

CARRIE　　It's weird this, isn't it? That I have to occupy your headspace. When you thought you couldn't get enough of me, here you are.

[beat]

	Could be like the ultimate chat up line, right? Or a last request from the scariest partner imaginable. Let me have a piece of your brain. Like a lock of hair. I'll hold onto it, keep it safe.
PI	It's nice, that. Keep on talking. It's a great way of readying yourself for it.

SAM prepares the syringe.

CARRIE	Well, it's quite exciting, isn't it? Pioneering, you could say.
SAM/PI	It is.

[beat]

SAM/PI	We want to reassure people that this is not a straight up punishment. We're not that kind of service.
CARRIE	Right.
PI	It does look a bit... threatening. Being plugged into the fraudulent network – not the best of realms. You'll be watched more closely there.
SAM	The crime system has vastly improved, hasn't it?
CARRIE	Since we had realms, now you can tag us all. A neat little game, isn't it? Laser tag. Peow Peow!

SAM/PI   Exactly that.

CARRIE closes her/his/ver eyes with a grimaced smile.

BLACKOUT

ACT 1

Scene 3

Monologue - Birth

PI It was only until I gave birth when I realised how separate we all are. Stupid, right? I was in the delivery room a long time - and my baby at the time - a little boy - the people who would pass by my bed, hungry for check-ups, an excuse to make the room free, would make little sniping jokes here and there. "Oh, you must be like a 5 star hotel, he's getting too comfortable in there", that's one of the more flattering ones, I guess. Didn't help the situation, of course. I was still floundering around, wanting to get this thing out of me. When it was a thing, you know what I mean.

I would think, you know. I had time to do that. Escape into my own mental space, even though he was in there with me, swimming around. How I was just another would-be mother, with the smell of birth in the air of countless others. That even with my own emotional stories, banal ones that these were just like template messages. Just change the names of the people involved. Of course it means more to me. But it's another child who's brought into this realm of entropy. A kid who, without consent, is kicked out into the fear and brilliance of life. A kid who will try and communicate with others, screaming, crying, laughing, talking, singing, anything to try and understand. Or vice versa.

They said I'd feel differently. You're seeing it from an objective point of view, they said, before the oxytocin kicks in. And it did. Right on cue. But hormones are written on the wind and water, aren't they? They can't always be there. We're not wired on instinct like that anymore. And even though I helped to make him, I grew him inside me - I will have no idea of what he's really thinking. I'll get an inkling, I'll get that women's intuition they say so that I'll feel calm. But it'll be nowhere near. I'll produce another line who's disconnected with the other till we're all lined up and we just need that one push. A domino line just waiting for it. Unless we can close the gaps in-between. Something like that.

ACT 1

Scene 4

CARRIE is standing in the centre of the stage. The director/actor can decide how Carrie/Lan can be played out in order to differentiate them.

(LAN)   You feeling ok?

[beat]

              Let's just talk it over.

CARRIE shakes her/his/ver head in refusal.

              You've got to talk to me sometime.

CARRIE   Pity.

[beat]

(LAN)   Look, Carrie. They linked me to you. I keep telling you/

CARRIE   /and I keep reminding you for a reason. It seems like you've forgotten why you're here.

(LAN)   I'm taking on these minds because that's what's needed. I'm pioneering this program.

CARRIE   Pioneering? And what am I? A glorified frigate?

(LAN)   For a positive reason, for policing those who/

CARRIE	/Taking us on - that sounds right. If you wanted advice on policing us, Lan, you have a crap way of doing it. A little too late, don't you think?
(LAN)	I know how it goes. I want to understand you. This network I've stepped in. To make a difference. All I want to know is/
CARRIE	/how I am. Equates to how do you stay put without killing yourself?

[beat]

You don't need to be a group mind to know that. But no, you want to alter our rhythm. Our patterns of thinking - to be like the "good ones".

[beat]

What are the good ones, in your opinion?

(LAN)	Isn't it obvious?
CARRIE	It couldn't be less obvious if you tried.

[beat]

One of the great things about group minds that you chose to meld in. Come on then, out with it!

(LAN)	Fine. People who haven't committed crimes.

CARRIE starts laughing.

(LAN) Is that too hard to understand?

CARRIE Talk about being vague! But anyway, it's not up to you, is it?

(LAN) It's having trust.

CARRIE It is. You're scared of what you've already entered. The hivemind of "vagrants", or whatever you call us. You're one of us now. Trust me, if you weren't, we'd make things a hell of a lot harder for you.

(LAN) I understand that. I just want to know how it feels. Your experience.

CARRIE Our experience, you mean.

[beat]

Free. It feels free. One network, many minds. Well, without you, it was.

(LAN) Now look at who's being vague. I could have heard that from any footage.

[beat]

CARRIE The mind stretches, right? It's not a little fencing round pins. It's a tapestry.

Whether it's rich and vibrant is any group's guess. The thing is, it needs something to stretch into.

(LAN) That's all you can say?

CARRIE That's all we need to say. We're not advertising here. You've already made the deal. It's time for you to live it out.

(LAN) It's just hard to believe. I mean, I heard your... Carrie's... interviews and you do sound different. But the same voice. It's just hard.

CARRIE People change. You don't need to be a hive mind to know that.

[beat]

Since, you know, this is a two way conversation, I'd like to ask a question, if I may. The vagrant hivemind at the mic. If we're into calling each other by our old names, what makes you a worthy leader, Lan? Why do you think you can handle us?

(LAN) I think my past records speak for themselves.

CARRIE Is that it? The problem's when you have nothing but statistics from a past life. Policing individuals. Nothing else to go by? Stats win robots. We aren't that yet.

(LAN) How do you even know anymore?

CARRIE What was hard about being a singular was that you had your identity in everyone else's hands. Something to bounce off. But once you're the mirror, who cares anymore? We know each other inside out.

[beat]

Listen. It's hard to find that path, that thread of stuff. But hey, it'll come in time. It's not innate, right? It's on the job, you know. And others did it, sure they did. I'm still here.

[beat]

There's nothing wrong with us.

BLACKOUT

ACT 2

Scene 1

"Monologue" - Lovers

PI, SAM and CARRIE are standing in a triangle. With each line, they break apart and come together. (The director can choose to emphasise or de-emphasise the physicality of this scene).

PI/SAM/CARRIE There are only so many minds I can love.

PI and CARRIE walk to the middle of the triangle. They kiss.

There are only so many kinds of love I can possess. And why can only you feel the effects of my kiss? Or is it yours?

CARRIE and SAM kiss.

I love you, you I love. It makes no sense but all the sense in the world. But it can't work like this, right?

[beat]

The world has created complications because we simplified things before.

We have to keep up. To write the damn world anew.

[beat]

> When locked in a particular coupling group though. Coupling. Made for two. Other half. Even better half. Whatever that was. No more allowed for that. Accepted sometimes but distasteful. Like we weren't capable of being loyal.

[beat]

> But to let others into this network, I don't know. How much is too much too soon?

[beat]

> Now that we carry us all in our minds and bodies, I feel like we have more to lose. One link cut and we're all snuffed out. Like that. Maybe that's what love is.

BLACKOUT

ACT 2

Scene 2

A trial scene. LAW and SYNE are sitting at a table.

SYNE	It's research.
LAW	Yes, carried out by you. Just you. Just one.
SYNE	I am aware of that.
LAW	They're not going to let you do this. I hope you know.
SYNE	It's not hurting anyone.
LAW	Hurting anyone? Do you hear yourself? How would you know who it's hurting?
SYNE	You don't know the extent of the research, do you?
LAW	No, we don't.

[beat]

Simply by existing as a singular, you're at a disadvantage. Sorry, but that's the truth. You don't have the empathy to survive in society.

SYNE	Simply by existing? Bloody hell, you do discriminate, don't you?
LAW	Levelled out biases. Extrapolating social norms, behaviours/

SYNE /How many minds are you?

LAW Makes no difference.

SYNE Think about it. Before everyone's absorbed into everyone else - it'll be how many. Not just the fact that you've created this community. It'll be the number. Or does that not worry you?

LAW We'll deal with that when the time comes.

[beat]

SYNE It might come sooner than you think!

LAW The point still stands, though. You're the one who has chosen not to meld into the network, expressly.

SYNE Not everyone got married in the/

LAW /this is something different. You have chosen not to meld in light of your recent development, i.e. your research.

SYNE You don't all talk like this, do you?

LAW Explain.

SYNE Well, if you think about the law of averages - surely you don't talk like that all the time? Like some of you would talk differently - or is that levelled too?

LAW We're in a damn trial here!

SYNE   You could've fooled me. Things have gotten very... minimalist in style, let's say.

[beat]

LAW   How long have you been here?

SYNE   Since birth?

LAW   Yes.

SYNE   Well, I was brought back into consciousness a few times, if you know what I mean. Not brought back, but brought forward. Different bodies, different identities, different times. You know the drill.

LAW   How many times?

SYNE   And that's not offensive?

[beat]

I'm old enough to know what I'm doing.

LAW   Age isn't an indicator of anything. That's thinking the old fashioned way.

SYNE   I'm glad we agree on something.

LAW   The last two identities you had were investigating "exotic matter" in your old words/

SYNE   /quite literally. Yes. It was.

[beat]

> Look. Can we just cut to the quick here?

LAW Right.

SYNE It's like playing chess against one hundred minds. How much calibrating do you have to do just to move forwards?

LAW You're thinking of those old fashioned games to mimic that. Different brains/

SYNE /Yeah, I know all that. It's just that I never knew quite how the brain developed in that way.

LAW Maybe you should change your research topic.

[beat]

> You see, this is what we're referring to.

SYNE Care to let this person here know?

LAW You're clearly unstable.

SYNE Is that such a bad thing?

[beat]

LAW It wastes time, yes. To think that one character wants power from everyone else.

SYNE You think it's all about power?

LAW Individuals are inherently selfish. Hence the word.

SYNE Well, I remember when minds were like that. Even before the earlier models, when all were singular. You'd get this floating mass of qualia and your brain would struggle to wire it all together. You know, for the right narrative to be unearthed. Take it how you will.

LAW Narrative?

[beat]

SYNE You've got to get the right people in your party. Not one of you know this nursery term?

LAW When you've stopped your own offensive nature/

SYNE /you still follow along, don't you? You miss the old orgy of thought tracks?

[beat]

LAW We'll give you time to consider. If you don't change your position on mind melding or your research in order to make it transparent or to terminate it completely, we'll have to confine you.

SYNE Confine me?

LAW   Do you need this explained?

SYNE   Different contexts, social connotations. I don't have to explain that, surely?

LAW   We lock you up.

[beat]

SYNE   (*laughing*) You lock me up?

LAW   Either that, or we can just track your brain wave patterns. We have a delightful video archive if you want that explaining.

SYNE   Really?

LAW   We don't make the rules. We hand them out.

SYNE   Clearly. Maybe you're worried about me gaining power because you have none to speak of.

[beat]

           So that's it?

LAW   You're seriously asking that?

SYNE   No torture chamber?

LAW   What kind of dystopian worlds have you been in?

SYNE   I've been... around, let's say.

[beat]

LAW Well, what's great about this system, which you'll find out eventually, is that the power is in our court. We could easily have you tortured. But the thing is, you aren't a problem. Not really.

SYNE Then... why all this?

LAW We are a small hivemind designed to sort out with minor issues.

SYNE And is that an issue for you?

LAW What, a person who's trying to blow up the world? More clichéd than whatever's been floating around in your little mind.

SYNE Sounds like the trolls are tolling the bells at the moment. A little mind wouldn't get that far.

[beat]

LAW If you're trying to... cause dissent amongst us about your judgement, you're not doing a good job.

SYNE Bit of a mouthful, isn't it? Cause dissent?

LAW Is this what you thought would happen? That you were summoned here for a bit of torture? The old waterboard, the phobia box, right?

SYNE   The phobia box? On what documentary was that?

[beat]

I have been tortured. Many lives ago. If you want, I could set it up. Cry a bit. Get people watching you if that's what you want?

LAW   Hiveminds are desensitised to that sort of thing.

SYNE   Really? All of them?

LAW   We've all watched things.

SYNE   I don't find that levelling biases. I have experienced it.

LAW   We know what it is. We won't use it. And we definitely wouldn't if you wanted to.

SYNE   Really?

LAW   This is why we are a small hivemind. A sensible one.

SYNE   And that's why you're policing the small cases, in their opinion.

LAW   It's their opinion. We have no need for it. It's not our concern to rise up in the ranks of a continuously changing system.

SYNE   Wise.

[beat]

> But I can tell you, I'm anything but a little case.

BLACKOUT

ACT 2

Scene 3

Monologue - war

CARRIE Everyone took it in a different way. Some took it on themselves as a large body of people – after all, we were weapons ourselves. Our guns were just extensions of ourselves. Like claws, like teeth. We just had a head guiding us, leading us into the abyss. But how do we feel about it now? I don't pull apart the weave, the pattern of impulse, but I add textures to it. Layers of living, of adapting back into life afterwards. Coming back to them all, knowing how much and how little to tell.

The stress, the trauma, the guilt of surviving when others haven't been so lucky... they're passed on. Not through genes, but through the raw neural networks. Or maybe they're the same? Who knows? We don't know who drives the vehicle now, or whether it's all of us.

It's in all of our networks. It's more... visceral than film. It's an embodied experience. It's like those dreams that are grounded in reality. We know not to do it. Not to bring them to life. Unless we absolutely have to. I remember when I was a singular. We'd have the silence, a time for reflection. To animate the bones of our memories to what we've seen, contact our ancestors, our witnesses. And it didn't work – years of anti-propaganda could do nothing to still those drives for power, for control. But now it does. Now it does.

ACT 2

SCENE 4

CARRIE (LAN)/SAM/PI are on the stage.

CARRIE   You don't question them.

SAM   Of course not.

[beat]

CARRIE/SAM/PI/   You shift all the time. Skin, hair, eyes, just like a sandcastle breaking down and building up again.

[beat]

    You find something new everyday. Something from your past.

Different sounds play in the background - it can be a soundscape of a beach, an army scene, wedding, garden, childhood. They overlap.

(LAN)   All I saw was the gleam of the knife and/

CARRIE   /All I had was time/

PI/SAM   /You thought you had.

SAM   And then everything went red.

CARRIE   Did it go red?

PI/SAM/CARRIE Sometimes the things you watch, they way you read things. They change your perceptions. It could have been red.

(LAN) Magenta?

CARRIE Pedantic much?

PI/SAM/CARRIE Doesn't change it though. You decided this path. Why don't you acquaint yourself with where you've gone? Timelines. Past the digital screens. The rawness of now.

SYNE comes on stage. PI/SAM exit.

SYNE Sandcastles? Looks like I've already spread my influence around.

(LAN) Fat chance of that. I lived by the sea.

SYNE Well, now, so did I.

[beat]

(LAN) I remember one time well. I was lying down by the sea, pebbles scratching my back and my sides, feeling more alone than ever. A friend of mine, Sophie I think her name was, had moved away and/

SYNE /her name was Sarah.

[beat]

(LAN) What?

SYNE	Her name was Sarah Cunningham. You were in Copa Cabana, craving the attention that she had for running away and thinking how you could attain it for yourself/
(LAN)	/No! That's not true!
SYNE	Memories aren't the most reliable things. Anecdotes, even less so. You did live in the Copa, didn't you?
(LAN)	I did for a while, yes. I did live in other places/
SYNE	/You don't have to give me any more information. I'm seeing if you knew.
(LAN)	You're making me out to be a/
SYNE	/child? We all were, once, Lan.

[beat]

Yes, I know. They know. It's a big step to take. One you can't reverse. Once you've stepped in the circle, there's no going back.

(LAN)	I can't take this.
SYNE	You can. It's just that you won't.

[beat]

The thing is, Lan, is that you joined this connection to police them. But all you've done is become them. You've not done it to fit your purpose. They wanted to be connected to feel a part of somewhere. They didn't join with any delusions of grandeur. They were unfulfilled with their lives and society as it was. They might seem small to people, but that's always been a personal thing. For whatever reason you choose, you have to be willing to shun the idea of self – and want to take on the life of a true community.

(LAN) So what is your purpose? To dip in and out of our minds? To think one is more than many?

SYNE I am the example of a true community. A legacy of many lives. I am many people in one.

(LAN) I may have difficulties connecting. Mentally. But at least I've accepted myself into their neighbourhood. You won't commit at all. They'll know this.

SYNE It's not a question of commitment. After all, you've been linked onto Carrie's network, but still trying to be an individual in the process. It's not working, is it? You're not Lan anymore. You're Carrie and you're not Carrie.

[beat]

>There's a right way and a wrong way. I'll show you how.

BLACKOUT

ACT 3

Scene 1

Monologue - Loss

SAM		The more people we know, we take, we talk to, the more we lose as well as gain. Of course, that has to happen. Being connected just means you feel it more. You're on the constant edge of the abyss. You know everyone. You know everything. From a human viewpoint I guess.

[beat]

		Or are we that anymore?

		We don't know who'll be first in the net, do we? We can sense, but that's just a little buzz of neurons rattling round like loose change. Just one day – you feel the gap, the space around it. Negative space. Or is it like forgetting? Will we no longer mourn in the same way? Has it already happened? Am "I", whatever that means, still here?

ACT 3

Scene 2

CARRIE (LAN) has her/his/ver hands around SAM. PI is next to her, trying to stop the attack. CARRIE (LAN) is completely out of control.

PI/SAM	No... stop it. Stop it!
(LAN)	Why the fuck is this happening?
PI	Ask that for yourself.
[beat]	
SAM	Let... me... go...
(LAN)	I can't! I can't!
PI	That's no... fucking excuse!
[beat]	
SAM/PI	It's because you can't let yourself be wired. You're letting the other consciousness's become dominant.
PI	Great! You're so high and mighty... yet you can't even release someone...

CARRIE (LAN) starts whistling.

PI   Oh hell. That's the sign. Just fight it.

CARRIE (LAN) breaks free and slumps to the floor.

PI	I can't believe you put yourself forward for it.
(LAN)	It'll get better with time. I will.
PI/SAM	What, like teething problems? More like a frigging cannibalistic nightmare!
SAM	She wasn't a cannibal.
PI/SAM	How do you know? No eating humans on her record?

[beat]

> Impulses. They all turn to... mush... when they're put in another frame.

(LAN)	You think that?
PI	Results are nothing on paper. They don't realise that.
(LAN)	So what are you going to do about it? Are you going to reject me?
SAM/PI	Is that a threat or a suggestion?
(LAN)	Transparency.

[beat]

> What sign is it?

PI	The whistling? It's one of our consciousness's who used to erm... put it lightly... strangle.

(LAN)   And they would whistle?

SAM   Keep the mind calm or something. Stop her from going too far.

(LAN)   It's not...

SAM   Not...?

PI   Come on!

SAM   It's not a murderer you're harbouring? A cannibal that's using your same mind pan?

(LAN)   Fuck's sake! It's not... you, is it?

[beat]

PI/SAM   Yes. And it's also you.

SAM   And you thought it would be that simple? After all that persuasion.

[beat]

PI   I was upfront about what I'd done in my past. What I might have been called on.

(LAN)   But how many... how many of you don't I know about?

PI   There's no self. Never been one. It's just even more obvious.

[beat]

	For one to have slipped into the aether, the existential nonsense has been heightened... into a load of crap. No bathos, no siree. Contexting patterns an' all that jazz.
(LAN)	Have you... what?
PI	That's all ya got. Words. Memories. Both of 'em aren't exactly legit, right?
(LAN)	Trying to confuse me?
PI	Don't need to.
(LAN)	So who are you then? What are you?
PI	I'm nobody and/
SAM	/everybody/
PI	/and when everyone is absorbed, they'll realise/
SAM	/Nothing has changed/
PI	/Just that it's clearer. No stones will be cast. Let she the one without sin, right? Or he, of course.
[beat]	
PI	We all know what we've been through. You have to, to really know each other.
(LAN)	What's your point?

PI	Ah, the old times. They used to share them around campfires, enough alcohol that every spoken sin becomes a beautiful blur.
[beat]	
	I don't even know if it was the old me or another version, but who cares now. I was ashamed – well, no, that was wrong, I was made to feel ashamed when I slept with a "married" person. Paralysed to act. I slept with them when I was a singular. Of course, those things were frowned upon. The vulgarity of fucking, especially when you haven't signed all the wedding contracts? But those times make us up. Or something. Now they're barely a grain of dust on the Savannah. What a lovely word.
(LAN)	So you had an affair?
PI	Oooh! How old fashioned. It'd be nice to have the retro tinge to our group.
(LAN)	So I have to share headspace with an adulterer?
PI	We're already there, aren't we?
[beat]	
PI/SAM	That means nothing now. Marriage was a way to fake closeness. And look... look at this!

PI	It's a way of being a pioneer, right? You get to write things from scratch.
(LAN)	But all of you are damn sinners! All of you!
SAM	And you're blame free, is that right?
[beat]	
(LAN)	Compared to you, yes. Yes I am!
PI/SAM	You chose to become us. Full of vagrants, as you call it. Never mind who Carrie had. Do you think she/he/ve knew/
SAM	/She/he/ve didn't have a choice/
PI/SAM	/That makes no difference. She/he/ve didn't know what she would get into either.
	That's the joy of it. You never get to know someone... until now. Nothing will shock when that happens.

BLACKOUT

ACT 3

Scene 3

Monologue - Work

PI You'd think employers would latch onto it, wouldn't they? A perfect force.

In the old days, it would be a dream. Number crunching, all keys inputted like a glorious symphony at the right time. No stopping for day and night. 10 minutes in between shifts a liability. Toilet breaks... human rights.

[beat]

But they haven't needed that for a while. Except those who campaign for robots rights – and you see where that's going, can't you? But when the robots program the robots without human aid – well, then the problem's well and truly on your hands.

PI/SAM/CARRIE Well and truly.

PI, SAM and CARRIE bring boxes onto the stage.

Cultivate your garden, no matter what. There's not much else left on Earth, so let's enjoy it when we can. Feel needed in that old fashioned way.

BLACKOUT

Act 3

Scene 4

SYNE is on the stage. Projections of humans bustling past are projected onto her.

SYNE   It's like that film. The wizard peddling his wares behind a giant mask. I forget what that is. No hivemind to call up. Just an old set of archives, wedged under my cortex.

[beat]

They know what it's like to be alone. A singular. We were all born singular – And all I've done is stay that way. I'm not the only one. It's just that they make the illusion of loneliness. That's the drive. The drive behind money, behind all that other crap. Loneliness with yourself. With everyone else.

[beat]

Just stay silent. Feel as though you belong to something. A wandering satellite.

BLACKOUT

ACT 3

Scene 5

LAW is standing in the centre, facing the audience. SAM and PI are standing in two corners.

SAM/PI	The body?
LAW	Yes.
SAM/PI	Could you clarify that for me?
LAW	The body, the corps, the corp...

[beat]

> The thing with the head and the thing that breathes and... you're taking the piss, aren't you?

SAM/PI	We certainly wouldn't.
LAW	Right. The flesh and bone.
SAM/PI	Why would you be interested in that?
LAW	In that? Have some bloody respect!

[beat]

> That's what it's like, isn't it, talking to murderers?

SAM/PI Aren't you supposed to be...? I don't know... objective? Not being offensive?

LAW	Offensive!? You... corrupted this woman, Lan Willow. You put a frigging sound bite in her/his/ve brain like a bloody teddy bear, didn't you?
SAM/PI	Corrupted? That doesn't sound right.
LAW	You've flooded her/his/ve brain with someone who doesn't even trust you? How can someone be more corrupt than that? Just for some information, right?
SAM/PI	Are you right?
LAW	These bloody hiveminds!
[beat]	
	If she/he/ve's not corrupted, why can't we talk to Lan? She/he/ve's not here now, is she/he/ve?
SAM/PI	Wrong.
LAW	Talk about being in denial!
SAM/PI	She/he/ve"s not dead. If we're going by file terminology, she/he/ve's being rebooted.
LAW	We've gotten a call. We need to see her/him/ver or the body, if that's the case. Or are you bloody pranksters?
SAM/PI	She/he/ve left her old mind, yes. Her/his/ver body is recovering. Her/his/ver mind is

	expanding. But she/he/ve"s here. You can talk to her/him/ver through one of us.
[beat]	
LAW	So we have to make a phone call? Use your arm as a fucking receiver?
SAM/PI	How old fashioned! But yes, your old technology can't track it, you can't prove it. Doesn't change anything for us. But it does to you. Well, at least... it should. It's the beginning of a new era.
LAW	Right. We're not getting anywhere with that attitude.
[beat]	
	You're coming with us.
SAM/PI	We wouldn't ask for anything else.

BLACKOUT

ACT 3

Scene 6

PI and SAM are standing on the side, having been linked by SYNE. SYNE and the LAW are centre stage.

SYNE I woke up like this. Woke up like this. That's what they said to exaggerate this idea of natural beauty, right? But it's true.

[beat]

How long does it take for you to really acclimatise to a reality? Waking from a dream, slipping to another one? I mean, this is all kindergarten stuff. Teamwork - well, that's the only option, increasing nowadays. No such thing as solo work. Well, one objective, right?

LAW Seriously, how long is this meant to go on for?

SYNE/PI/SAM You want it cut out, right?

LAW We want to see your evidence. Not your life story.

SYNE/PI/SAM That is the evidence.

LAW It hasn't been so far. We can't wait to rip into this argument. Like a frigging patchwork quilt.

SYNE But for me it felt like a reverse snobbery, that kind of thing. You know, that you feel that you're so superior for not wanting to belong to one arc, like/

SYNE/PI/SAM One of me is worth ten of you/

SYNE /And I didn't want to think that. But it was thrust on me. I wasn't the one who made that choice.

LAW But you're telling me you've what... absorbed all of these individual selves?

SYNE/PI/SAM I have put a part of myself – my conscious wiring – into every one of these selves.

LAW We refuse to believe it.

SYNE/PI/SAM That's what we are. You saw what I showed you. This is just another step on the ladder. The way we can perfect these neural networks.

LAW But why... why would you say this? If you were an individual, we'd have just locked you up.

SYNE/PI/SAM You can't lock us all up. Prisons used to be overcrowded before. We are an individual. We are Syne and we are not Syne.

LAW That doesn't make sense.

SYNE/PI/SAM It will make sense. And that is why I didn't lie.

SYNE I could attribute my findings all to myself. But that would be a lie, right?

LAW So... from groups to the individual? You're regressing?

SYNE/PI/SAM Just listen to the feed.

SYNE Groupminds were the big thing. Co-ordinated people crawling around, respecting each other's space. Easier to monitor. Easier to handle. Everyone follows the other.

LAW Writing this fancy speech isn't going to help anything. Drawing out time like this. Self-indulgence. That's what it is.

LAW presses a button.

LAW We've decided to stop recording. State of exception.

SYNE Oh, but why?

LAW Why? You've messed with the system. We cannot allow it to be transmitted. We have come to a deliberate decision.

SYNE looks around. PI and SAM are silent.

SYNE   We're all working on this big project. A liberation of self altogether. If we all know the way to escape this world, then we'll know not to use it. To not harm each other.

[beat]

You've used it all wrong. All of you.

[beat]

It also explains why I've had to show you all these damn clips, right? As they told Carrie before she connected - there's only one way you can communicate. Things go missing. Gaps. That's what Pi said. What Sam said.

LAW   So this has been one stupid advert for world destruction?

SYNE   That's what you've been doing. Groups with separated mindsets. The spaces are still there. Good for art, not for real life.

[beat]

Actually, no.

LAW   No?

SYNE   It's good for art because you can empathise with so many viewpoints. I've felt the minds of murderers, lovers, artists, scientists, bankers, the lot. Sometimes they can be more than one. Ah, being facetious. That's a bad trait that so many of us have.

LAW But you're controlling them! Think we're just paper frigging dolls? You're playing... you know...

SYNE It's not a game!

LAW You're policing them, plaguing them with your thoughts. You uploaded part of your damn mind in there. The parts you want.

[beat]

SYNE Sounds like how these group minds have worked, really.

LAW I don't think so. Empathy works when you're on the same level. You've tried to raise your level in spite of this fear.

SYNE Fear?

LAW I don't see why you cannot wholly commit to your cause. You still want to be a head. A head to a larger body of people.

SYNE I'm not quite sure what you're getting at.

LAW Oh, you do. We all have our "dirty little secrets" Syne. Except they're not anymore. When you're on the network, nothing is secret. Nothing is sacred and there's

	something about it that you're holding back/
SYNE	/but you're still here. Enforcing.
LAW	It's because of people like you.
SYNE/PI/SAM	Like all of us?
LAW	Right. You're using these humans as puppets. We just hand out the rules. You're acting them out through bodies.
SYNE	They signed up to this. This freedom factor. If we work together on this project, then we/
LAW	Freedom factor? You have the keys to all of... their minds and you're just a landlord? What's that to do with freedom? That's just sheer power you're craving.

LAW draws a gun.

SYNE	Oh! Oh really! That's what this is? A lawyer with a firearm?
LAW	That term is obsolete. We are a peace enforcement unit. Where the laws are being drawn up constantly.
[beat]	
SYNE	You make me sick. In a rather amusing way.

SYNE turns back. PI and SAM aren't moving to her aid.

        I don't understand! I'm asking you to/

LAW   That's the problem with singulars. They have what they want from you.

        Why would they need to protect you?

[beat]

SYNE   You... no... you...

LAW   They can't relate to singulars anymore. Neither can we.

SYNE turns to face them.

SYNE   But don't you see? I need to be separate, because... because... I can see ahead for us. I've been through so many lives, and you know this. I'm a hivemind all my own and I...

LAW   A hivemind all your own? How touching.

PI/SAM   And utterly selfish.

[beat]

SYNE   What? But I thought that/

LAW   /Not everyone has to speak out. If you were truly a hivemind, you'd know that.

[beat]

> Why do you think we found you? Things have changed since the old days. We're more than a chorus. A band of willing leaders for you. It's group preservation. When you're out controlling your group, you don't even know who's in it. Who you've kept and who you've discarded.

As the next speech occurs, SYNE is walking backwards. The LAW advances with the gun pointed on SYNE. PI/SAM stand on either side of SYNE.

PI/SAM We made this bond because of the information. Because of having you as a leader. We have that now. Everyone lives on in the minds of the other, the other and the other... (*continuing*)

BLACKOUT

A Gun Shot.

ACT 3

Scene 7

Monologue - Leaders

SYNE is on the screen, while LAN walks on stage.

SYNE V.O   In this day and age, you still need a contingency plan. When you've lived as many lives as I do, you realise how important it is to backup. Spread yourself thin and hope that the pieces join up again.

(LAN)   It's not enough. It's not.

[beat]

SYNE V.O   Yet still you focus on just me, don't you? Listen, really listen. All this is still going on in your head. Frequencies. Just more of them. Stronger waves. A bigger capacity, a larger playground to roam in. Yet you still focus on me.

[beat]

    A leader fails because they only had one perspective. One viewfinder. I've had many. We've had many. I'm just a guide that's travelled through many times, in one container. But that's all about to change.

[beat]

(LAN) If we're talking to you, there's something wrong. If you don't know who we are, something's wrong. Something's amiss with you and you and you and you.

[beat]

> We can't erase our language. We think in impulse and strain it through words. It's our own personal alcohol. We don't want to erase it entirely, but we want to limit it.

[beat]

> The more we understand...

(LAN)/SYNE V.O The less we talk. The more we feel, the less we hurt. The more we rely on empathy, the less we suffer.

LAN builds up a wall out of bricks around the stage. The characters in the projection follow suit.

PI/SAM/LAW/CARRIE (LAN) /SYNE V.O If you are not on our side, we will understand. We will not build walls to drive out, but to protect the group within. Those who wish to fulfill our project. Our potential. Democracy is not for everyone.

[beat]

> We know what we need. We are SYNE and we have come to conclusions. It's not a

device in the typical sense, but through an individual's lens, it would be. For us, it's a boundary broken. For good or ill.

[beat]

Isn't that what it is, at the end of all of this?

[beat]

One network. One world. We are SYNE. We have spoken.

The soundscape plays again.

BLACKOUT

END